AMONG THESE SHOPPING CARTS, YOU FORTRESS,

AMONG THE PLASTIC BAGS YOU AFFIRM:

LO! THE LIGHT FROM THE DESERT TREES

DOES NOT SPEAK IN NUMBERS, COSTS US NOTHING.

AHSAHTA PRESS.....THE NEW SERIES......................

.........................#74......................BOISE, IDAHO...

THE MARKET WONDERS

Susan Briante

Ahsahta Press, Boise State University, Boise, Idaho 83725-1525
Cover design by Quemadura / Book design by Janet Holmes
ahsahtapress.org

LIBRARY OF CONGRESS CATALOGING-IN-PUBLICATION DATA
Names: Briante, Susan, author.
Title: The market wonders / Susan Briante.
Description: Boise, Idaho : Ahsahta Press, [2016] | Series: The new series ; #72
Identifiers: LCCN 2015049403| ISBN 9781934103647 (pbk. : alk. paper) | ISBN
    1934103640 (pbk. : alk. paper)
Classification: LCC PS3602.R485 A6 2016 | DDC 811/.6—dc23
LC record available at http://lccn.loc.gov/2015049403

FOR GIANNA

TOWARDS A POETICS OF THE DOW   1

OCTOBER 1–DECEMBER 16

October 1—The Dow Closes Down 9509   15

October 6—The Dow Closes Up 9731   16

October 14—The Dow Closes Up 10015   17

October 15—The Dow Closes Up 10062   18

October 22—The Dow Closes Up 10079   19

November 25—The Dow Closes Up 10464   20

December 7—The Dow Closes Up 10390   22

December 16—The Dow Closes Down 10441   24

MEDITATION   23

THE MARKET IS A PARASITE THAT LOOKS LIKE A NEST   27

MAY 10–JULY 23

May 10—The Dow Closes Up 10785   39

May 14—The Dow Closes Down 10620   40

May 15—The Dow is Closed   41

May 17—The Dow Closes Up 10625   42

May 26—The Dow Closes Down 9974   44

June 4—The Dow Closes Down 9931   45

June 14—The Dow Closes Down 10192   46

July 2—The Dow Closes Down 9686   47

July 23—The Dow Closes Up 10424   48

THE MARKET IS A PARASITE THAT LOOKS LIKE A NEST 47

MEDITATION 55

OCTOBER 8—DECEMBER 19
October 8—The Dow Closes Up 11006 61
October 18—The Dow Closes Up 11143 62
October 24—The Dow Is Closed 63
October 29—The Dow Closes Down 11118 65
November 12—The Dow Closes Down 11192 68
December 11—The Dow Is Closed 69
December 12—The Dow Is Closed 70
December 19—The Dow is Closed 71

THE LESSON OF THE NEST
The Market as Composition 77
April 19 79
July 8 80
Addendum 81

MOTHER IS MARXIST 83

NOTES 109
ACKNOWLEDGMENTS 112
ABOUT THE AUTHOR 113

When one is a woman, when one is writing poems, when one is drawn through a passion to know people today and the web in which they, suffering, find themselves, to learn the people, to dissect the web, one deals with the processes themselves. To know the processes and the machines of process: plane and dynamo, gun and dam.

MURIEL RUKEYSER

An economy is a system of apparently willing but actually involuntary exchanges. A family, for example, is really a shopfront, a glass plate open to the street.

BHANU KAPIL

TOWARDS A POETICS OF THE DOW

Every day has a number attached to it. Great additions, subtractions. This is not just an aesthetic problem (see Ashbery). There is a "natural impulse toward the boundedness of closure." The bell rings, trading stops. But the world is "unfinished" (Hejinian). Both the rivers and their banks are moving. The poem remains incomplete. The trading day long over.

I do not believe if I follow the Dow I will find nirvana, but I often check the numbers, sit for meditation.

Even when we think we are at the end, there are decimals.

* * *

When the Buddha touched his finger to ground at the moment of enlightenment, all the leaves fell from the Bodhi tree. It is February 10, 10:04 in the morning, the Dow falls to 12194. The present poetic strives toward total awareness, incessant recording.

Ravenous as a black walnut tree, roots sucking at the sewer line, the Dow touches everything: the taste of our water, color of our sky, torque of our engines. It is February 10, 10:15 in the morning, the Dow at 12203 is rising. The poet—like the trash tree—uses all of it.

A poem moves as does the Dow influenced by a variety of factors and events: mergers, oil spills, revolutions, suffering. Sometimes what does not move tells the story. I like poems that go to prisons and coal mining towns. I like poems that act as archive or a view to Elizabeth Street. I admire circuitry and cosmology. I write with a power industry dictionary on the bookshelf behind my desk, a copy of the King James, a guide to Texas trees.

Poems should evidence some degree of control, but poets should be a little volatile. The poem is a high-risk investment, a long-term commitment. Like a big dirty city, it should make you feel

a little uncomfortable.

It is February 10, 1:11 in the afternoon, the Dow falls to 12197. The poet wants to remind the Dow that the bird has something to teach it about falling and song.

* * *

The theoretical physicist says, "I've always wanted to find the rules that governed everything."

The theoretical physicist says, "Deep laws emerge."

I have a friend who asks about "truth" in poetry. Whenever he does, I want to send him a valentine on musty pink paper. He lives in a Mid-Century modern house with Mid-Century modern furniture carefully culled from vintage stores and eBay. He owns an old mahogany stereo cabinet, jacked up so you can listen to an iPod through it. That's the kind of truth in which I am interested.

Plus the silence, plus the static.

Charles Olson writes, "no event/is not penetrated, in intersection or collision with, an eternal/event."

To which I offer this corollary: no event is not penetrated, in intersection or collision with the stock market.

I wish more poets would write about money.

* * *

The New York Stock Exchange began when brokers met under a buttonwood tree in 1792, the year that Blake wrote "Song of Liberty," the year Shelley was born. Charles Dow created the Dow Jones Industrial Average, representing the dollar average of 12 stocks from leading American industries, on May 26, 1896, six days after the U.S. Supreme Court introduced the "separate but equal" doctrine.

Now corporations have the same rights as people. Why can't poems? I nominate Robert Duncan's "Poem Beginning with a Line from Pindar" for president, Frank O'Hara's "Having a Coke with You" for chairman of the Senate's foreign relations committee, Gwendolyn Brooks' "In Montgomery" for attorney general—although the House will not approve it.

Brenda Hillman explains, "Shelley wants you to visit Congress when he writes/a *violet in the crucible* & when he notes/ *imagination is enlarged by a sympathy.*"

Bernadette Mayer asks us "to show and possess everything we know because having it all at once is performing a magical service for survival by the use of the mind like memory."

Blake reminds us, "For everything that lives is Holy!"

* * *

And there is this: When you make the poem, you can hear the swish of dollars washing down the sewer line, second by second, you can hear the stock ticker ticking away.

* * *

Farid rests in child's pose on the living room floor. Gianna sleeps in her crib. The Dow closes its eyes. In the park across our street, nothing blooms. Winter grass the color of a lioness. My warrior. My tree.

After the fall of Mubarak, reporters talk to tailors on Cairo streets. They broadcast video of doctors who treated the revolution's wounded. People write congratulatory notes on their lab coat sleeves. We love the look of magic marker on white cloth. But no one tells us how much money we've sent the dictator over the years. How many more receive our checks? There are bigger equations, larger alphabets, scripts from which I want to unwrite myself.

In 1994, the artist Mark Lombardi began working on a series of spindled drawings that graph relationships between business and government elites, tracing paths of financial meltdowns and mergers, shady deals and convenient bedfellows. The poem, as well, can spin webs.

The archive is wide. The poem accepts yellow leaves, guide stars, a crop failing, my milk coming in. We need the aerial photograph and microscopic slides as well as something beyond our personal viewfinders. Not a ball and chain of cause and effect, but a tendency toward pattern, implication, investigations of grief and ecstasy.

The artist Mark Lombardi worked in pencil.

The poem and the stock market welcome speculation.

* * *

What a drag it is to be among people who fear art because they think it mocks them. The tree is nothing but the tree. Or your mother. Or the nation. Bank of America, Merck, Pfizer. Nothing changes from generation to generation except the thing seen. Rusty backhaw, golden rain tree, 3M, Alcoa, AT&T.

We record noise, interference, outliers, error.

On February 10 the Dow closes up at 12273, poised to snap a winning streak, may fall tomorrow on Cisco. Characters ticker between us. Both the river and its banks are moving. A bird rests at the end of every winter branch plotting its own flight path.

Across the dateline, markets open.

* * *

OCTOBER 1 – DECEMBER 16

In the dream, I queue with a pane of glass in my hand.
Next to me: a child and a mirror.

Then we stand at the edge of an accident.
I pick up a sliver of windshield, place it on my tongue.
The glass tastes like cold stone and dirt and I love
the way it fractures in my mouth.

Glass often indicates a strong psychic or intuitive ability.
Broken glass predicts change, not necessarily beneficial.
To receive cut glass means you will be admired
for your brilliance and talent.
To dream you eat glass signals vulnerability,
confusion, frailty.

$9+5+0+9=23$ $2+3=5$
$5 =$ freedom, adaptability, unpredictable travel, abuse
of the senses.

In a Sufi proverb, the bear must deal with 20 obstacles,
each one of them involves pears
because the bear adores pears.

....
In Revelations the angel commands John the Divine *Rise and measure!*   And thus begins
a prophecy a litany of calculations *40 and 2 months 2 witnesses 200 and 3-score days*

Not everything is about:
this body, this 5-fold aggregate based on clutching
the mocking bird is a stranger in a strange country

the past—like the path of a mocking bird through sky
past utility poles, power lines—
has entirely disappeared

        (but I want you here)

....
2 olive trees 2 candlesticks in a singe of data John like a physicist scavenges for God *3.5 days,*
4 and 20 elders, 12 stars, for the prophets to measure is to signify and separate (we diversify,

I bleed a little, peyote tea waits in the refrigerator,
a Ferris Wheel spins and spins at the fair,
after the miscarriage we search
for rings with missing stones, unmatched earrings,
sell our gold, ride the Ferris Wheel bigger
than the one in Paris,
my parents pray for us, I play Dylan's "Spanish Boots"
over and over, watch a sunroof fill with night,
like seeing a film of people I recognize
but don't really know,
Schuyler says you can't get at sunset
listing colors, between the liars' trees and shopping carts
we buy a house, cry in bed, leave
the child unnamed
pink lemon pearly blue white

....

we financial officer) as in the story of the Samurai who falsely accuses his servant Okiku
of stealing 1 of his 10 delft plates, his words spreadsheet, she inventories: 1 2 3 must be

What if I write it all down, track it, if I consult tickers
and windows, measure blood flow, monitor the rise and fall
of my accounts, the tarnish of leaves,

will a veil tear, will a web sparkle dew-strung, a rope bridge
between the dead-living-unborn?

Can I feel these numbers in my hands
like Whitman at the rail of a ferry?

The Dow rises above 10,000.
My dog scratches his ear.
A lamp buzzes   on its timer. Rains
clear and the cold
arrives. The unborn
keep their distance.
I make a dinner of brown rice, butternut squash and kale:
some [thing/event] or my 3000
          nerves bristling in the air.

....
4 5 6 mistaken 7 8 9 counts again, her master will spare her if she fucks him, an equation
she refuses, he throws her down a well   a well is a chamber of calculations, an ear

The Dow rises and sinks, floats
like oil on the surface of a sea, an albatross
feeds her offspring pieces of plastic,
my *almost* gone more than a month now, for what wrong
did we feed it?
      The air says: winter,
most of the time says: gray slips of winter without snow
fixed like a nail, says: I clench
a coal October sun in my fist, slip
it into a pocket of horizon or carry it
in my throat and leave it there
accumulating no interest.

....

a labyrinth of bone a darkness so seldom our habitat, whence Okiku endlessly counts 1 2
my genre is trauma 3 4 an obsessive ticker 5 6 my genre falls 7 8 from office buildings 9

We stuff steel wool
into cracks along the roof,
spray silicon in gaps,
night blackens windows,
until we feel clasped
as in "here is the church
here is the steeple,"
but our friends
stay away, 3 days
after the poet's death
his email came,
a light touch,
he wrote, he wanted
to make the room light,
we hardly have enough, cut
a hole in the kitchen wall,
you can learn about time
from brick, beam, board,
what remains unmapped
is more than we know,
whenever in doubt
win the trick, the kitchen wall
does not teach missing.

       After midnight an owl

....

Okiku screams like mid-level managers in the 1930s in times of stress as before a fall
or angel or robbery at gunpoint in the back seat of a taxi we see in hyper-reality, innumerable pixels

sets the dogs barking *come out,*
come out, I am dying,
the owl shuts an eye
like the unborn,
wrapped in winter
gauze, we bring
headphones wherever
we go, we leave
the shades drawn,
      window closed,
another way of killing
what gets caught
between glass and screen.

....
(my god, my billfold), a national debt clock ticks off the trillions, numbers jump and flip, the
minute hand slips as a doomsday clock ticks down our fate, *arithmomania* the poet said his mind

I watch weather,
monitor the troubling of trees,
a stranger comes to my door
a cloud that shouldn't be there
hangs overhead like a half-lit log,
smoldering sunset—
don't roll on me!
an R.E.M. pop song post *Reckoning*
would be the last thing
I hear, the stranger
the last thing I see,
what happened
to the lead singer
who used to sing into his hair?
      Dead,
the Buddhist would say:
we die every minute
when we open like a door to the next
      as the stranger stands at the threshold
smells of liquor
asks me to buy some magazines
from the lettered present:
December 7,
Tom Waits's birthday,
Delaware Ratifies Constitution,
....
burned with numbers, how many bricks in a wall, coins in a purse, glasses on a tray, a hook, a
burr in thought to explain why vampires stop to tally beans or seeds dropped on the ground

"Islamic" New Year,
  which sounds like a mistranslation
  reminds me of how I thought I
  heard you rattling the gate,
  Ya'aburnee
  from the Arabic,
  the phrase has no equivalent,
           it means bury me
  because I love you so much
  I do not want to live
  to see your grave.

....
but a hungry child simply grabs and eats,   our ticker tells a story of national precarity,
numerical OCD, John's angel commanded *Measure!* Okiku screams, my gunman barks *Give me*

Someone maps the unmapped sectors of cosmos
the Himalayas look nice from cloud
Tibet, Nepal, Bhutan
        I record what I can, document

start at the edge of a piece of paper
cross a track.

Sometimes we don't feel the burn of a space heater
until hours later.

A child came and left like a stranger at the door.
There is no map for her coordinates.

So we try again on the twelfth or thirteenth day at the edge
of a lunar cycle, a blank piece of paper

$1+0+4+4+1=10$
$1+0=1$

$1=$ Creativity, independence, originality, ego,
the unity of all things, symbolized by a circle

....
your wallet or I'll fucking kill you! to submit to another's accounting is to surrender is to default
in a taxi where I hand over my money (so Google mapped, so market crashed) not counting

MEDITATION

In the PartyStore/PierOne/Target/Kohl's parking lot,
find a desert willow among the shopping carts,

walk around it sunwise repeating:

I am the avant-garde, I am the avant-garde, I am the avant-garde

repeating:

DIY, DIY, DIY

Imagine a chart of median family incomes
as big as the parking lot—
use it to determine where to abandon your car.

I default, I default, I default

Your mind is a blood blister rising on your thumb, a ladybug.

Among these shopping carts, you fortress,
          among the plastic bags you affirm:
Lo! the light from the desert trees
does not speak in numbers, costs us nothing.
Here, as in a butterfly garden, everyone crawls before flight.

THE MARKET IS A PARASITE THAT
LOOKS LIKE A NEST

The Market scowls,
crosses the street against traffic, settles, hovers
over a spread-sheet with his administrative assistant
as if it were an infant, sleeps in another bed
after $3\frac{1}{2}$ years of marriage,
can only sleep on half the bed
after 43 years of marriage, sees a coffin
in a shop window, grows nostalgic
for shop windows on crowded city streets
where men made picture frames, repaired
television sets, piled tools in doorways, nursed
machines to roast and grind coffee,
operated a printing press. The Market wants to apprentice,
cannot apprentice, looks like a nest in a tree. The Market
is a parasite that looks like a nest in a tree, howls
through the ventilation system, hairless, blind, a newborn
calf sleeping on your chest, the curdling Market
whose milk has come in.

The Market wonders where the soul goes,
decides that God must be a cripple to make the rest of us
feel whole, remembers a trip to Mexico
when he was just out of college.
O the beggars in clown paint! O the girl he never wrote!

Jacaranda, jacaranda, jacaranda

Cheap purple leaves dirtying the sidewalks.

A street named for revolution.
A street named for insurgents.
A street named for reform.

Nights when church bells rose to Aztec temples

Like the soul?

At the hostel, she told him
a body must train to hold the light of the spirit.
They fucked listening to the Rolling Stones, burning candles.
God, the Market loved Mexico and the Rolling Stones.

Then the Market had kids and it was all profit
margin and technostructure
roller-blades for a few years,
mostly he all but forgot his legs
it must be okay to be nothing
but sight after a while
all this over here, that over there
the packing slip, the manifes-
toes, arches, heels, calves
like his doctor told him, relax each muscle
against all this shimmer:
grass sequined with difference,
butterflies trembling like addicts,
in a cornfield the violet is weed.

—What does pink and yellow make?

The Market's youngest daughter asks him.*

—Orange, he says.

—What does chocolate and cookies make?

—Your favorite treat.

—What do all those numbers make, Daddy?

The Market looks up from the *Wall Street Journal*.

—The ones in your hands.

The Market sighs.

Why does anyone have to make anything?

*Can you ~~imagine~~ *smell* the Market picking up ~~his~~ *your* daughter ~~from school~~ *in its teeth* dragging *parts of* her *body* across a ~~playground~~ *landscape* touching everything ~~he~~ *it* touches as if it were a screen? See how reflective the glass, how *he* is an *it* is a *we*.

The Market always feels so heavy
by the sea, weighted by a thousand
sacks of coins impossible to sort, to let
go without hemorrhage, to lighten
would be to dissolve not like an ocean
against a horizon but to sink
from continent to silt to slam
down taking walls and foundations
root systems, swing sets, whole cul-de-sacs
the Market worries he is nothing
but a pile of stones when he feels so much
inside of him slipping in and out of place
and is somehow expected to speak
from one throat.

Eight three three nine eight three three nine.
Eight three three nine eight three
        three nine eight.
Three three nine eight three three
Nine eight three three nine eight three
three nine, three nine, three nine
eight three three nine eight three three nine eight
three three nine eight three three nine eight three three
—nine eight three three nine eight three three nine eight three
three nine eight.

MAY 10–JULY 23

Black walnut tree cuts a path
up the mid-spring sky
the mind only carries you so far
a dog licks his empty bowl
over and over a decade
goes in real wages
while you increase productivity
the poem says cultivate
your infinite   anxiety
is a hole
in your neighbor's wall
shaped like a crow
the poem tells you to open
like a bank account
stand like seedling
against a granite sky
the black walnut tree says patience
where the prayer flags used to fly
the poem casts a shadow
in the shape of a tree
the tree circulates
its own currency
and does not claim
the unseen hand
belongs to god

....

In *Revelations* John measures the walls of New Jerusalem (144 cubits) walls fix the promised
in a promise of containment   our friend the addict says it's hard to get up in the morning,

The more I move the less I feel the baby.
I track her stillness.
And what is feeling without document?
The body is not cyborg. Winter will come
with its iron tongue
lick the year clean
reveal   wires through trees.
I know, too, there is water above us
methane below. The body endures
a sickness of proximity
awaits the ill story
of winter when I'll tell the child
yes, there were leaves.

....
stay clean, slide day against day, beads on an abacus, make simple calculations, in folktales
a spell like a market algorithm changes fate, a stepmother turns 11 princes into 11 swans

after James Agee

Sometimes I think there should be no writing here just my checkbook registry,
envelopes of receipts, browsing history, photos uploaded, list of status updates,
texts received,

the postcard of a tornado someone stuck in our gate advertising a roofing
company.

Our view gets wider once we fix the gutter and awning.

And Gertrude Stein writes: "After all anybody is as their land and air is. Any-
body is as the sky is high. Anybody is as there is wind or no wind there."

As a child I was forbidden to climb trees. As a child I could lose whole days,
wake up in a hospital bed with a deep broad ache, pills that tasted of mint and
paper. As a child I learned to connect my cursive letters, memorize multiplica-
tion tables, divide and carry what was left over.

Zeppelins floated through Stein's sky,
now we carry the Zeppelins.

The tents grow nearer; the cop inside us
pulls out his mace.

....
tells them *Fly out into the world and make your own living*,   their sister must spin nettles
into sweaters to break the curse,   every theory is fabric and calculation,   I measure from

39

Farid says he wants to be a family,
he adds, by which I mean I don't want you to die.

In Arizona, police pull over a man
for rolling through a stop sign
and ask him to show proof of residency

I want to tell Farid
since I was a child I have dreamed
of feeling like this, by which I mean safe.
Instead we talk about the baby.
She will cry a lot the first days
her skin in clothes, darkness
and light, touch and taste
will shock her to tears.

I just read that somewhere.

In Dallas, temperatures filibuster spring.
The Dow "eyes" jobs, uses
a variety of special characters,
while we find a hole in the birdfeeder,
collect box tops for a water bottle,
enter contests for a green home.

....
middle finger to elbow (15.25 in.) knee to hip (18.75 in.)   any tailor, any archeologist
would know this,   every system binds in Europe men raised cathedrals 144 cubits

Suzuki compares existence to wrenching
a droplet of water from a stream.

In this year of our drought
all of our favorite photographs
were taken under cloud.

....
to bring the dimensions of heaven to earth, numbers taken literally like pills (our addicts, our
prophets) or spells as in a folktale when the sister of the prince-swans is sentenced to death

Some days it is easier to talk with the dead than the living.
On your side of the Atlantic you sleep and I am lonely
thinking of how this talk might wake you.
I check my departure gate,
want to swim in information
grammarian, orator, servant, lender.
The birds sound like Texas
mornings, coins feel heavier.
I don't have a name for these Old World trees.
The Bible calls the tree both good and evil.
But we know it's not the apple
when the branches cause our undoing,
putting this here, that there—you in our Texas bed,
me in a Spanish airport, the dead with no return address
hanging over us like a thousand leaves.

....
for witchcraft   carried to the stake before she can finish her youngest brother's sweater
she throws 11 sweaters over 11 swans who become 11 princes but 1 carries a swan's wing

My heart drops a note, systolic, beats for you,
Jim James sings on the radio, the radio sings:
yesterday the Dow rose, a flood. Outside

not a leaf moves,
I can't feel a single branch,
let alone the oil in plumes, feathers

of a thousand estuaries. How do you separate
an individual from life? Experience
washes up on the coast, you stand

on levees, on barrier islands.
Try to pull tar from feathers,
like Whitman try to sympathize

with each drugged wave:
You there, impotent,
loose in the knees

bully sympathy, landlocked,
compromised. Let Al Green sing,
I can make it rain when I want to.

....
in place of an arm, his sister becomes queen, the end is meant to be happy,   my dissertation
adviser told the story to remind us when writing: *You can live with 1 arm* but can you live on 1

The names of 62 birds are listed in dry erase marker
what we do and see exceeds conceptual categories

what counts as real depends upon the dry erase board
joins in a continuous loop with information technology

sympathy as feedback/dialogue
sympathy in the comment box

yellow bird (unnamed) at the feeder (likes this)
a squirrel eats pears from the tree

bluegreen dragonflies fly by the tomatoes, release
the long lag between   between thought|sentence

what at first appears to be a Graph Theory problem
is a simple Longest Common Subsequence problem

just as yesterday's seminary students with thick library books
suggest an unwillingness to invest in certain claims

to the bird I seems bigger than I am
to the sky—another matter all together (3 people like this)

....
income? every sweater is a series of patterns Revelations spirals in sequences 7 eyes 7 heads,
7 horns 7 days to world-create, a number of completion   and 3.5 that number halved, number

Physicists say the universe might be a projection
on the edge of a screen, shadow by the door
or the boundary between the Muskogee and Cherokee
nations more nothing than anything else
smash the smallest parts to see if nothingness breaks
but there must be another way, a reason
in the cosmic order to necessitate human existence
an equation to explain the little arrows
at the ends of my fingers, plate glass above all that I do
and you hold the grease pencil
and you move the shipping containers
across the horizon like a sentence about to be said:
this morning I saw the word "dog" in the hair
left in the bathtub and no matter how I turned
I could not get it to read "god"

....
unfinished, of demons,   every system patterns   and we learn   to see at half glance
(half prince/half swan)   our ancestors scoured the ground   for game, nuts, berries

I want to purchase a little silence
as if prospecting in the old west,
glean what might be raised
from such soils or panned from this flow.
If the eye were emptied, what would I see?

A shape I have already settled upon?
Prayer without robes? My mind
stuck in its gears
makes it impossible to read
a trace of light on the patio
where the dog finds the tiles cold.

Let the light grab whatever it can.
Let the quiet come
when the branches still
then the cuffs, ankle bar,
home insurance, car payment,
the cold grip of everything
that keeps us standing.

....

and when they looked up (eyes scaling a wall) they saw grains and forbs of light in the sky,
in time we counted stars, but first we drew pictures, told stories, to find our place in the night

THE MARKET IS A PARASITE THAT
LOOKS LIKE A NEST

Know thyself, the oracle said.
But by what measure?
Archeologists will know me better,
the Market thought,
as he took out a measuring tape
from finger to elbow, elbow to shoulder,
not even lovers learn these
intimate calculations. An obituary
lists dates, ages, numbers
of children and grandchildren
survived by such a horrible phrase
that brings to mind
a group of wounded passengers
staggering across a tarmac
wreckage, sirens,
waiting to be saved.

From the airplane:
great tuffs of forest, subdivision, field
must be rice paddy, water-covered, deep
in crop, evergreen, bluegreen. The Market
imagines those are shallows. He can be
certain of the water filtration plant, its pie
-graph slices, the curved roads of adolescent
neighborhoods, shoulders of teenage girls,
only here he recognizes them
as strip mined, dust lake
must be manmade, sky hazed,
first day of summer, patchwork of earth grown
into a field of cloud, no horizon to be seen
and this terror | beauty
of something that has no limits

Dogs bark down the road, dogs bark
out back all night
with some crickets and cars.

At dawn—birds from window to window—
the Market showers,
            water makes him feel present.

Inside: a season of silence except for the ceiling fan
with its *tsk, tsk, tsk*.

Walking his grandson to school, the Market notices
dinosaur stickers above the doorway
of a boarded-up house on his street,
a dog chain wrapped around a skinny pine tree.*

---

* The Market cardinals in the tree we cut back year after year, I sit in a red plastic chair trying to get
  within an inch of its screeching.

The end is woven into the beginning,
a name sewn into the brocade of your evening
coat, a sore inside your throat

—even the Market knows this.

We know nothing but this living
the Market thinks, not to go on forever
without a beginning, middle, end
but a chance to learn something
else, a single breath
beyond this story, a book he saw
with paint-covered pages,
paragraph by paragraph erased,
whole neighborhoods,
friends, memories
turned white space, blind spot, skeleton, poem
in place of a thick life of prose and no one
to teach him how to read it.

MEDITATION

5 objects are placed before you:
one as tall as you feel when you lay
        your daughter in her crib each night,
one as heavy as your daughter's cry.

What would the largest object hide from view?
What will not be concealed
(dumpster, Dollar General Store, mountain, moon)?
Which objects are gift? Which existed before you?

Something lands in the corner of your eye.
Instead of words, you white out
        thoughts.
Let them burn like dirigibles in the sky.

Send the ash to the last person who lent you money,
to a sparrow in flight through the black walnut tree.
The sparrow clicks like a Geiger counter in the leaves,
your daughter's hunger swells.

Your mind is a plastic bag full of water to ward off flies.
The flies don't come.

OCTOBER 8—DECEMBER 19

In the dream I visit my dream Newark, which looks nothing like real Newark, but I know its landmarks: park, brown brick castle, cathedral with fog, lake somewhere beyond, shuttered lighthouse, brownstone where my mother grew up.

I meet a poet who is frail and gray-haired and won't stop talking in red skirt, yellow blouse, carrying a canvas bag with pieces of construction paper sticking out, and nothing she says makes sense. The young man with her offers a despairing glance, and we follow her past lighthouse, lawn, fog into a building down cream-colored halls through a door in the back of a closet to a room where students sit around a seminar table. She pulls out a yellow notebook, takes her seat at the head and begins:

> *Always a story, no matter how avant-garde you live.*

....

A pattern imposes form on cloth   and on the fingers of a teenage girl under factory light
who picks, spins, measures, a circuit   behind a screen, brand on a body, current routed,

Static on the television makes rain
on the roof
after the jerk and swaddle of morning
we peck at our notebooks
consider the ditch dug
up the middle of our lawn
$4000 gone   down the sidewalk
two krishnas swell in saffron robes
rain owls sing in the alley
are you awake too?
only the rich burn candles
not a question of greed but motion
as in capital or the poem
or my child who wants to keep rocking
I nurse her, wait for sun, click refresh,
and both of us want to feel
bigger after I write this

....
stitched across countries: *42 months 1,260 days, 2 olive trees, 2 lampstands, .27 of US households live
in "asset poverty" without savings to cover 3 months of expenses,* an auspicious number, a laptop

My daughter tugs my pant leg,
takes my hand, walks me round
the house, living room, kitchen,
leaf clung   we vine
down the bedroom hall
morning-glory blue
      in the midst
of drought, in this season
of protest parks
I come across a photograph of a cop
swinging his baton, his badge
easy to read   the caption includes
his name, address, phone number,
email, in the comment box
someone's going
to order 20 "nasty-ass" pizzas
to his house, someone's going
to get his social security number,
cut his electricity, blow
his fucking head off,
we are already naked
Steve Jobs tells us

....
powers up, everything patterns: *12 stars, 7 heads, 10 horns, 7 crowns*   and outside the Green
Zone of our 1st-world economy   *3.5 days, .1 of the city, 7,000 people, 2nd woe, 3rd woe,*

and Steve Jobs is dead
things fall away—
remember the little bomb
with the error message?
— in the face of death
                it's easy to hate
the part that swings a baton,
hard to know how far we'll get
this early this late   season
my daughter takes her first steps
toward the window
with a view to the drought park
red I want to show her
because the park is green/gray
but all I can conjure
is a blood blister
on my finger, my ladybug,
in this mess of October   leaves
don't change   they fall
grass grows grocery-bag beige
three hours south
of us   people
take to the streets
to meet the rain.

....

7th angel   a rose moans through prickly pear   thorn loves thorn,   in drought, a rose
petal falls to shrapnel, the desert light   trains us to love the pallid   survival flaunts

I.

to make one thing of me, writes Rilke
or to "work me, Lord" as Janice sings
like a field song, mocking
-bird variations
for which I can find no equivalent, and no sooner
       have I written this down then
I want to post it on a screen where I can see all
manner of bodies burned, burdened, crushed
by the weight of factories, here stitched into this night
gown, look up from this screen, which holds all manner
of soldiers before/during/after their tours of Afghanistan,
drones, the actress
like some lesser martyr
who cuts off her breasts,
now flickering before me, cold candle, a fire
I cannot feel hums through me particle sure as any unseen
cancer or cracks in the wall of the garment factory
("work me, Lord") covered in paint

....
all around us like a national soccer team, whatever is weak   welcomes,   John was exiled
to Patmos, his story spirals in repetitions, extends a fabric of waves and particles and string,

11.

why must man always take on things
map galaxies, name particles
while factories burn, ash rises to satellites,
the question I carry around like a locket
with a dead child's hair, the question
of dead children comes
with mine
begins "the world
which is economic system does not care"
and in the wilderness beyond which is particle attraction
and distraction I slip from the grip of garment
factory fire, to ask
over and over:
            can you take it all
in, galaxy after galaxy, open your eyes sky wide
through love or force or training?

········ ········· ···················· ······ ················ ··········· ············· ·············· ······· ············ ···········

a portfolio of catastrophe that spirals round like Blake,   Ginsberg,   Kocot,   McSweeney,
I never read biographies of famous poets   because they make me anxious about money

III.

let's remember this sky
and underneath the factory workers like a thought
that dark matter thinks, a fluttering candle,
let's place ourselves beneath the hood of night
you can't gate this, razor wire, Guantanamo Bay this
the hospice nurse says rest
in the space between breaths
                                    let there be space
in your gaze, let there be nurse
before you post your status update, wash
clothes, pull up the rug,
like my status update, my revolutionary status update

measuring signifies and contains,   of the 7 beatitudes in Revelations the first begins *Blessed*
is he who reads: folktale, verse, portfolio, spreadsheet, the American dream   is fairytale:

Gold leaves fall from the black walnut in torrents,
then the rain in a lesser denomination.
I look up from a poem, refresh my home page:
the congressman says God will save us from climate change.
South Carolina trips on the Constitution.
Rudyard Kipling claims the real American
is *unkempt, disreputable, vast*
—as Texas?

      It is 80 degrees in late November, O nation,
and the sunset over the liquor store/gas station
knows there's very little it can attempt.

....

say you want to ghost, say you want to go rogue from this set of data   where there is no
cloud, no cover, I don't walk much lately   but know exactly which streets hoard shade,

"Cannonading is not agreeable, but it is bearable," Gertrude Stein writes, "but bombing from above and not very high above is mightily unpleasant."

Drones sound like the hum of monks at prayer, are insects living in honey, can come from anywhere, out of any sky

which turns the color of worn cotton at dusk, rough hem of winter when leaves and mockingbirds hush, shadows litter the sidewalk before an empty house, fully lit, and across the street a woman places something on her porch.

Stein says during the occupation the countryside was easier than city except for the gas and butter rations, and we already feel occupied but our feeling doesn't have a tank at the end of it.

On the internet, photographs of German police who take off their helmets and march with protestors in solidarity or arrest 340 protestors or serve as escort.

The facts matter. "I'm hopeful," writes X in the comment box. Stein says her occupying Germans were polite, "very correct."

One does not feel safe

with analogies. What I think is moon is Venus, but I take a picture anyway. In this dim light it looks as if the woman bows at her doorstep.

....
between a shadow and myself   a theory, an exchange, my husband's Facebook status
proposes: "You know you are middle class when _____"

December 12—The Dow Is Closed

for Farid

Years later, my love, under glass
in the taxidermist shop in Paris
I remember green plumage,
a cat, no, something rarer, an ocelot,
a case of blue black butterfly wings,
a branch, on the way to someplace else
we passed a hotel with a plaque
for Vallejo (did he die there?),
took a photograph, what words can I use
to make you feel my love big
as a golf course, sky, cosmos, as the orbit
of the object formerly known as the planet
Pluto, which is dark and cold, and Death,
the best I can do is tell you,
I've got two poems left in Notley's book
and I know they will be good, but I am not
going to read them yet, this afternoon it snows
in Paris and the snow says rest.

....
there is a way/no way to be absent from the system.   *Unsubscribe, Unsubscribe, Unsubscribe,*
I put some of my life, my love,   in a space   between numbers,   .   between the values

if you want to catch the sun
you'll have to drive
down another street
my ambition's thinner
I watch my daughter's
chest rise sink
we raise children
who will die
look up
from the driveway
on the first night
of standard time
see an owl in flight
later he'll trigger
the dog next door
light one yard over
it smells like
drier sheets
or is that the sweet
of a new season?
      yesterday
on the toll road
I read a billboard

....
against which they are judged, I have set a ticker (tick, tick, tick,) like Muriel Rukeyser does
in "The Book of the Dead," numbers kill and crowd,   dive and ascend   stick like nettles,

about hungry children
($1 feeds 6)
today *Midwinter Day*
I stick a green paper
in the book
so I know
what to read
when you get home
keep the porch
light on   try to ward off
what's hungry
              try to record
with tenderness
light turn
-signaling
in the trees
we catch a glimpse
of sound
cannons in the park
scientists say the universe
tears itself apart
I watch our daughter
play with curtains

....

like burrs on my skirt sewn by some teenage girls in a foreign country with only the language
of numbers, *a mobile language of computations and rationalities that belong to the corporation* between

before the rush
hour traffic
         and when I write
about light in the trees
it's like   fuck you
a human being
killed by a drone
is still killed
by a human being
off the page
where roses bloom
in our backyard
ice covers the porch
wind closes the airport
you say that might be good
for surf
         I wonder if drones
have a pulse
on some screen
some one
to watch
a little line
break

....
us, my numerical vision makes me: prophet, addict, lonely,   my genre is national hunger *we*
witness the advent of the number…woven tight like a fabric with neither rips nor darned patches,

I don't want to settle
the mind
want to say something
to whomever
follows me #hashtag
off the page
and to my daughter
I want to say
we are all tired
and working too hard
on the market
on the floor
futures trading
is an awkward song
owl's cry bookmark
flaring curtain sunset
I don't know
       how to read this text
from the Tarot
I draw the pink slip

....
a trauma narrative repeats, the lesson of the nest is scavenge and weave,   a trail you follow
through a canyon as ocotillo points with bloodied fingers to a place where clouds used to be

THE LESSON OF THE NEST

On February 10, 10:04 in the morning, the Dow falls to 12194. Who swims? Who rafts or islands? Rivers rise like the Southern Pacific Railroad Company. Characters ticker between us; characters leaf. Both the river and its banks are moving

past a grove of southern trees. Mimosa, magnolia, osage orange. Our indexing makes trails through a forest of mind. Hot linked, jumpy. On the day William Carlos Williams died the Dow closed up 667. Branches

scrawl across a winter white sky. Black branch, yellow leaf. Sequined with difference. At the moment of enlightenment, when the Buddha touched his finger to the ground, all the leaves fell off the Bodhi tree. Religion

has the touch of a bird through grass. Wood duck, gadwall, northern pintail. On the day Robert Creeley died the Dow closed up 10540. The Dow closed down 1130 on the day Prince released *Purple Rain*.

You call a yellow leaf gold to stop a child's crying. Golden rain tree, rusty backhaw, sycamore, elm. A penmanship branches across sky, stiff as dialect, hard as the 14th amendment.

An eddy in a river makes a small cup of world. Hooded merganser, cooper's hawk, northern harrier. Write your headnote in the sky, like the court reporter, J.C. Bancroft Davis who wrote, *obiter dictum,* corporations have the same rights as individuals. It is sad

to be among people who don't read, who fear art because they think it mocks them. The river is nothing but river. Or your mother. Or the nation. Merck,

Microsoft, Pfizer. Draw water, carry firewood, bear this instant. In the prolonged present, you hear dollars tick. Leaves static. Leaves distract. On the day Robert Rauschenberg died the Dow closed up 12828. Water rushes over stones with a touch as light as a court stenographer. Winter branches scribble

obiter dictum. Nothing changes from generation to generation except the thing seen. Rusty backhaw, golden rain tree, 3M, Alcoa, AT & T. Hot linked and jumpy as the sunset over a gas station

and that makes composition, makes an index, makes a footpath out of yellow leaves.

I am no longer certain about the origin of things. My child does not sleep. So when I recalled the blond haired woman in the red dress playing a ukulele and my recognition—yes that's how you learn to play, with a humble fret board, smaller neck—I could not remember whether I had seen her on television or in a dream

nor could I find the bit in *The Autobiography of Alice B Toklas* about Picasso and Stein turning a corner in Paris to see the camouflaged tank; Picasso stammering something about it is we who have created that. His recognition before the tank was aesthetic not systemic.

But mostly I was interested in that turning

or the story about Petit Jean on a fishing boat who turns to a young Lacan and points to the glimmer of a floating sardine tin. Do you see it? He gestures to the object sparkling on the water's surface. Well, it doesn't see you.

Ten years ago when I left New York I gave up the guitar, so when I first saw the blonde-haired woman (wherever I saw her) I thought that I should have started with a smaller instrument. But as I watched more closely her intricate fingering, the finest needlepoint, I realized it was not a matter of ease but of tune.

An instrument might be a string of equations, technique, process, transaction.

I wanted to fall in love with a procedure, but I could not fall in love with a procedure because I could not always hear its song.

In the stop-start of morning, I look to take leaps, find a place to hold my daughter. Her accounting is small, and her morning is a tide that sand-shifts like traffic.

I wish we had Schuyler to meet us at the beach to add this up and turn away like gulls or waves or Olson to show us how this shift made land for our house and what's underneath before even the continents splintered apart.

It's not all mind, bodies

are different where they land and what they can do this deep in a year, this far towards shore, this close to traffic and waves.

And by daughter I mean any obligation and by mother I mean any tragedy.

First there is a moment, then a poem. A man hangs a ladder from utility wires, another witnesses on his front steps—which is artist? Over the beach an airplane hauls an advertisement for a hospital.

An invisible calculus exists
beyond the page, a second story
leaf tremble, that view exactly
with the powerline running through

I want you to see it *here* where I stop writing because my child calls to me from another room.

After my daughter stops nursing, my body continues to make milk and this spawns tender fantasies or wretched comparisons as in the last scene from *The Grapes of Wrath* when corporate farmers let peaches spoil on the branch while a young mother nurses a starving old man after her stillbirth.

Things rot. Markets make no exceptions. How many poems should I make this morning? My grandmother was a wet nurse.

While the mourning doves coo, I am reading Marx: capitalist, bourgeoisie, proletariat, aristocracy, millocracy, moneyocracy.

After the fall of the Soviet Union, the Cuban engineer told me water was shut off for hours each afternoon. Power outages lasted for days. Neighbors gathered at battery-operated radios, networks knit around scarcity and excess. Who were those other children who nursed where my father did?

For weeks after weaning, my breasts sting. I spend the day poem counting. One book gets you a job, two get you tenure. The poem machine turns factory.

The mourning doves aren't talking like it is 30 years ago, aren't talking like a family could live on one income.

When I was a child, the engineer told me, the revolution was the most beautiful thing. *La cosa más bella*. Then the engineer went hungry. Some critics claim Steinbeck's dying old man is capitalism is communism is our twentieth century Pietà.

Lack something long enough, and a market springs up like a peach tree straining toward the sun. Even the mourning doves know this—the lesson of the nest is improvisation.

MOTHER IS MARXIST

My daughter plays hide and seek with the white floor-length panel curtains in front of a window in our living room. Dusk traffics light, the light scans her. She is gold leafed in the curtain before the window.

Can't you see her gold?

* * *

"I do not know whether you have seen the building of the Metropolitan Company in New York. . . ." Charles Coolidge Read stated before the Massachusetts Legislature in 1895. "Go up to the directors' room where the floor is soft with velvet carpets and the room is finished in rich red mahogany . . . there you will find these gentlemen who think what a beautiful thing this child insurance is . . ."

Read insisted that from every block of marble in the Metropolitan Company building peered "the hungry eyes of some starving child."

In 1895, one could purchase a $10 life insurance policy for a one-year-old child or a $33 policy for a 10-year-old child for 3 cents a week. One and a half million children were insured in the United States in 1896. By 1902, that number climbed to over 3 million.

Advocates said the policies served as funerary insurance as well as protected poor and working class families against a loss of income at a time when child labor was common. Opponents, like Read, believed it provided incentive for poor or working class parents to neglect or outright murder their children for profit. Such opponents never questioned the ease with which they believed poor or working class parents might be tempted to kill their children. Actual incidents of infanticide related to child insurance appear to be rare.

Still, a writer for the *Boston Evening Transcript* declared: "No manly man and no womanly woman should be ready to say that their infants have pecuniary value."

* * *

When we lived in the two-bedroom house on a busy street on the fringes of a "good" neighborhood in Dallas, once every a couple of months I would hear gunshots, often on Saturday nights, usually late enough that I was in bed.

We purchased the house through the Obama tax credit program for first-time homebuyers, a response to the economic crisis of 2008 and the housing market crash. Because we could not afford to put 20 percent down, we had two mortgages, the second of which included a balloon payment.

We purchased the two-bedroom house on a busy street on the fringes of a "good" neighborhood in Dallas because we were trying to have a baby and the neighborhood had the best public elementary school as well as two Montessori charter schools.

* * *

The average per student expenditure for public elementary and secondary schools in 2012–13 ranged from a high in Vermont of $19,752 per student to a low in Arizona of $6,949.

* * *

The market scans my child, calculates pecuniary value.

Parents register and respond often seeking out places (the "good" neighborhood or private school) where a child's value is high enough in relation to the needs of others to make them relatively safe

or a parent may reaffirm existing market valuations.

And if the child is female or presents as female
And if the child is queer or presents as queer
And if the child is poor or presents as poor
And if the child is of color or ethnic or presents as of color or ethnic

a little spark of mica in a field of sand.

* * *

Pregnant women and new mothers have a heightened sense of smell and easily disrupted pattern of sleep.

* * *

One night after a particularly loud series of gunshots heard from the bedroom of our two-bedroom house on a busy street on the fringes of a "good" neighborhood in Dallas, Farid called the police. I don't remember what he said, what kind of injury we could have reported, what response we expected.

When we bought the house, we joined the neighborhood association. We also had the option of paying an additional $180 for "an off-duty police officer to patrol our neighborhood each week" as well as "answer our emails" and provide "special patrols" while we were away.

* * *

Per day, per pupil, per square foot

many parents may want to register and respond to the values the market places on their child, but a parent's own depressed value may leave her with scant time to challenge market valuations of her children, child, self.

"Boys are easier to raise than girls," my mother told me.

I feel my depressed value as a woman
as well as my surplus value as a white ethnic.

The consultant in the TED talk teaches me to stand bigger.

* * *

In 1908 a ten-year-old girl working in a mill made 30 cents a day.

In 1911 an eight-year-old girl shucking oysters made 30 cents to 35 cents a day.

An eight-year-old boy, who had been shucking for three years, earned 45 cents a day.

In 1917 a ten-year-old girl working on a tobacco farm made 50 cents a day.

As recently as 2014 the Human Rights Watch reported it remained "perfectly legal" in the United States "for a 12-year-old to work 50 or 60 hours a week in tobacco fields, as long his or her parents' consent and the work doesn't directly conflict with school hours."

* * *

Often the day after hearing gunfire from my bedroom of our two-bedroom house on a busy street on the fringes of a "good" neighborhood in Dallas, I would scan the Internet looking for some piece of news to link to the sounds. I never found mention of a shootout or injury or killing.

The gunshots existed as fragments in a storyline that seemed to have no relation to me, a non sequitur, a piece of conversation overheard in a language in which I had no fluency.

But those metaphors are wrong.

My legislative representatives cannot or will not pass gun control policy, my tax dollars support the purchase of surplus military equipment by police. The white imaginary criminalizes non-white bodies.

* * *

On December 2, 2014 the Dow closed up 17,879.

On November 22, 2014 the Dow was closed.

On November 20, 2014 the Dow closed up 17,719.

On August 19, 2014 the Dow closed up 16,919.

On August 12, 2014 the Dow closed down 16,560.

On August 9, 2014 the Dow was closed.

On August 5, 2014 the Dow closed down 16,429.

On August 2, 2014 the Dow was closed.

On July 17, 2014 the Dow closed down 16,976.

On March 22, 2014 the Dow was closed.

On February 16, the Dow was closed.

On January 28, 2014 the Dow closed up 15,928.

On January 16, 2014 the Dow closed down 16,417.

On each one of those days in 2014 one unarmed person of color (most frequently an African-American man, sometimes more than one) was killed in the custody of police according to information released by the NAACP in late 2014. This list is by no means exhaustive as no central agency tracks the number of police shootings or killings of unarmed victims in a comprehensive way.

* * *

From 2001–2011, Department of Homeland Security grants provided police departments with $34 billion to fund their militarization, making profits for military contractors and for-profit law enforcement training organizations

like special ops supplier Blackhawk Industries (founded by a former Navy SEAL), ThunderSledge breaching tools, Lenco Armored Vehicles bulletproof box trucks, KDH Defense Systems's body armor, like HaloDrop "flying robotic services for serious incidents and situations," D-Co, Leaders and Training LLC, like Innovative Tactical Training Solutions, like Winchester Ammunition.

Every altercation helps justify the militarization of police

and someone makes money makes money makes money makes money.

* * *

I want to teach my child to shed numbers like a skin in the summer, in the shimmering heat of the ever-warming summer.

* * *

We were able to afford the two-bedroom house on the fringes of a "good" neighborhood in Dallas because it sat on a street with six lanes of traffic separated down the middle by a small park or a large median of trees.

Most of the windows in the house were painted shut. Many rattled from the vibration of passing cars.

We kept a small padlock on the gate at the top of our driveway.

Before the padlock, men sometimes came to our door smelling of liquor selling magazines or asking to use our phone. Once I watched an old sedan lurch onto the sidewalk in front of our house. A woman shouted from the driver's seat while a man reluctantly exited from the passenger side, pieces of clothing flying out the door and window after him.

From the front windows of the house you could see cottonwoods, oaks, and black walnut trees. From almost anywhere in the house you could hear the traffic.

* * *

Mothers attempt to erase the integers, to move decimals, to point out discrepancies in the ledger, disrupt the protocols of exchange.

When the mothers of the victims of police violence march on Washington, DC,

when mothers in Central America set their children like paper lanterns

on a breeze,

when warehouses of children wait at our border,

Mother is Marxist, exposing as false and pernicious the mystification of capitalist instantiations of value, promiscuous relations of value and their violence.

Mother is not a biological or relational subject position, but can be an attitude of resistance before the market.

* * *

Underfunded public schools show their cinder block, reveal their district paint purchased from the lowest bidder, can't hide their too many desks, their too tired, their underpaid.

You see it in their lunch trays.

Private schools flaunt their walls of windows, famous architect library, flagstone pathways, full-time counselor.

In such places, children learn to read
their market value.

* * *

Scholar Viviana A. Zelizer explains: "Children's insurance began as outright bets among 16th-century European businessmen on the birth and lives of boys and girls."

* * *

A police officer flaunts his gun and in the amount of time your child is afforded to pull their hand from their pocket

you can learn their market value.

* * *

Value differentiates. Metaphor makes false equations.

When we talk about metaphor we talk about "vehicles," but metaphor can erase distance, conceal the mode of transport: the ride hiding in the wheel well of the 747 or the journey along a dry riverbed through the Sonoran night.

The work of all mothers is not equal, although the goal to challenge market valuations may be the same. The market exploits our attachments, makes its violent calculations. The market, mothers, divides and divides us.

And someone makes money makes money makes money makes money.

I want to slur the equations.

* * *

My love for my daughter is dumb and simple
all of my feeling focused, funneled
into the leaky sewer line
running down our front yard
from which the black walnut trees feeds.

* * *

Sentimentality is a shard from the shop front window of family. What sliver of American plate glass do you see?

I sympathize with the desire to throw a brick through a shop window and steal a television set.

But sympathy is never enough.

* * *

Children are not paper lanterns set on a breeze.
Imagine cutting off an arm to save the body.
Dear mother, you feel like the arm

* * *

In Tucson, we buy a 2–2 house in a "good neighborhood" with a neighborhood association. We no longer hear gunshots at night. We no longer have the chance to pay for additional police patrols or attention. We hope to get our daughter into a better elementary school than the one in our neighborhood through an open enrollment lottery.

Often we fall asleep to the sound of helicopters or planes taking off or landing at the nearby Davis-Monthan Air Force Base: the A-10 Thunderbolt II or the HH-60 Pave Hawk helicopter, the HC-130J Combat King II transport, the F-16C or F-16D Fighting Falcon.

The financial advisory giant Deloitte predicts continued decline in revenue for the global defense sector, with the U.S. defense budget "a key driver of this decline." Still Deloitte gave A+ ratings to stocks in this sector including Textron, Honeywell, Huntington, and Curtiss-Wright.

* * *

Unmanned aerial vehicles, better known as drones, scan the Sonoran desert for moving bodies.

There are no accurate numbers for the children killed by U.S. drones outside of our country.

Sometimes when I look up I can see the pale underbelly of the HC-130J Combat King II transport gliding over the streets of my neighborhood or the playground of my daughter's preschool like a hand passing over a velvet rug in the boardroom of an insurance company.

* * *

If we traveled far enough, we could find 1000 children waiting on the border, they were walking toward us.

"Towards a Poetics of the Dow" takes some of its references from William Blake's "A Song of Liberty," Brenda Hillman's "A Violet in the Crucible" (*Practical Water*), Lynn Hejinian's "The Rejection of Closure (1984)," John Lehrer's "A Physicist Solves the City" (*The New York Times Magazine* 12/17/2010), Bernadette Mayer's *Midwinter Day* and Charles Olson's "A Later Note on Letter #15."

The composition of the dated poems began in 2009 when I started recording the closing number of the Dow Jones Industrial Average. I let that closing number randomly guide me to texts: plugging it into Project Gutenberg, Bartlett's quotations, online versions of *Paradise Lost* and *Leaves of Grass* as well as various search engines. I allowed those texts to exert their influence over a series of poems—sometimes subtly, sometimes dramatically—in order to formally mimic the way the closing number of the Dow exerts an influence over our lived experience. As the project developed, I found other ways to let the closing number have an impact on the poem. For some, I allow the record of the Dow to serve as framing. For others, I allow its absence to serve as commentary on the serial project and production.

For "October 1—The Dow Closes Down 9509" I used numerology to find the indications behind the number 9509 as well as referenced a dream and a weekly horoscope.

Lines from "October 6—The Dow Closes Up 9731" take their inspiration from the Old Testament quotation "I have been a stranger in a strange land" (*Bartlett*'s quotation 9731) as well as from *The Way of Zen* by Alan Watts.

"October 14—The Dow Closes Up 10015" found a seed in Ecclesiastes 1:18 (*Bartlett*'s quotation 10015) and in a slippage between naming and knowing: "He that increaseth knowledge increaseth sorrow."

October 15, 2009 marked the second consecutive day that the Dow Jones Industrial Average rose above 10,000 since October 2008, the start of what of has been called "the current economic crisis."

"October 22—The Dow Closes Up 10079" makes slant reference to Isaiah 22:23, "Fasten him as a nail in a sure place" (*Bartlett*'s quotation 10079).

"November 25—The Dow Closes Up 10464" takes the phrase "When in doubt, win the trick," from *Twenty-four Rules for Learners* (*Bartlett*'s quotation 10464). The line "Come out, come out, I am dying" comes from James Wright's poem "A Message Hidden in the Empty Wine Bottle That I Threw into a Gully of Maple Trees One Night at an Indecent Hour."

"December 7—The Dow Closes Up 10390" took inspiration from the phrase "spirit and matter" from the title of the first chapter of *The Edinburg Lectures on Mental Science* by T. Trower (Project Gutenberg eText 10390).

For "December 16—The Dow Closes Down 10441" I used numerology to find the indications behind the closing number.

In the poem "May 10— The Dow Closes Up 10785," a Google search of 10785 pulled up a website for the "The Southwest Depository/Recycling Center" and set me off considering cycles, circuits, currencies, and trees.

"May 14—The Dow Closes Down 10620" refers to the quotation: "The iron tongue of midnight hath told twelve" from *A Midsummer Night's Dream,* Act v. Sc. 1 (*Bartlett's* Quotation 620).

"May 17—The Dow Closes Up 10625" borrows the phrase "uses a variety of special characters" from Project Gutenberg eText 10625.

"May 26—The Dow Closes Down 9974" references "The borrower is servant to the lender" from Proverbs xxii. 7 (Bartlett's quotation 9974). I began writing the earliest versions of the Dow poems in spring 2009 when my friend Craig Arnold went missing and was eventually presumed to have died while hiking in Japan. His death hovers over many of these poems.

In "June 4—The Dow Closes Down 9931," the italics in the fifth stanza refer to line 993 from *Leaves of Grass* (1855 ed). The poem also quotes the My Morning Jacket song "It Beats 4 U" as well as Al Green's cover of "I Can't Get Close to You."

In "June 14—The Dow Closes Down 10192," the phrase "at first seems like a Graph Theory problem, but it is actually a simple Longer Common Subsequence (Dynamic Programming) problem" comes from entry UVa 10192 on the www.algorithmist.com wiki.

The war story behind Bartlett's quotation 9686 ("I am here: I shall remain here.") hovers behind the poem, "July 2—The Dow Closes Down 9686," a reflection on softer boundaries than the trenches and front lines associated with combat.

"October 8—The Dow Closes Up 11006" makes reference to the title of Project Gutenberg's eText #11006 *The Book with the Yellow Cover* and a dream.

The poem "October 18—The Dow Closes Up 11143" borrows the phrase "only the rich burn candles" from a *Roadside America* story (#11143) on the Thomas Edison Memorial Tower and Menlo Park Museum. The quote comes from Edison.

"October 29—The Dow Closes Down 11118" takes inspiration from Rilke's "Spanish Trilogy" instead of the market.

"November 12—The Dow Closes Down 11192" borrows the Kipling quote from *The Americanism of Washington* by Henry Van Dyke (Project Gutenberg book #11192).

"The Market as Composition" takes the line "Nothing changes from generation to generation except the thing seen" from Gertrude Stein's "Composition as Explanation."

In the "Ticker" the italicized sections come from Revelations, Michel de Certeau's "The Practice of Everyday Life" and "The Assets and Opportunity Score Card" (2012 by Jennifer Brooks and Kasey Wiedrich)

"Mother is Marxist" draws on the following source texts: Spencer Ackerman's "41 men targeted but 1,147 people killed: US drone strikes—the facts on the ground" (*The Guardian*, 24 November 2014); Jo Becker's "Child Laborers in America in 2014" (Human Rights Watch, 17 Sept. 2014); Lewis Hines' photographs and documents from the National Child Labor Committee's Collection; Rich Juzwiak and Aleksander Chan's "Unarmed People of Color Killed by Police, 1999–2014" (*Gawker*, 8 Dec. 2014); Jaeah Lee's "Exactly How Often Do Police Shoot Unarmed Black Men?" (*Mother Jones*, 15 Aug. 2014); Andrew Schulz and G. W. Becker's "Local Cops Ready for War With Homeland Security–Funded Military Weapons" (*The Daily Beast, Newsweek/Daily Beast*, 21 Dec. 2011); and Viviana Zelizer's "The Price and Value of Children: the Case of Children's Insurance" (*American Journal of Sociology* 1981).

ACKNOWLEDGMENTS

Some of this work first appeared (sometimes in an earlier form) in *1913, Cannibal, Canteen, Colorado Review, The Common, Connotation Press, Diagram, Eleven Eleven, Evening Will Come, Everyday Genius, Mandorla, Matter, Poets for Living Waters, OnandOn Screen, Sentence, Spoon River Poetry Review, Sous les Paves, Stolen Island, They Will Sew the Blue Sail, Third Coast, The Volta: Medium* and the Academy of American Poets' Poem-A-Day website.

A selection of these poems was included in the limited-edition pamphlet, *$INDU or Ghost Numbers, October 1, 2009–December 16, 2009*, published by Longhouse Press, as well as the chapbook *The Market is a Parasite that Looks like a Nest* published by Dancing Girl Press.

The poem "December 11–The Dow is Closed" was printed as a limited-edition postcard and broadside by The Headlamp.

"Towards a Poetics of the Dow" and "The Market As Composition--Addendum (After my daughter stops nursing)" appeared in the anthology *The Force of What's Possible: Writers on Accessibility & the Avant-Garde* from Nightboat Books (2014). An earlier version of "July 2—The Dow Closes Down 9686" appeared in the anthology *Devouring the Green* from Jaded Ibis Press (2015).

My heartfelt thanks to all of those editors.

Gratitude as well to the Djerassi Resident Artist Program, Fundación Valparaíso, and the Virginia Center for the Creative Artists for time and space.

Additional thanks to Sam Ace, Rosa Alcalá, James Hannaham, Phil Pardi, and Roberto Tejada, who read this work and helped it find its final form. Special thanks to Janet Holmes.

Special thanks to Farid Matuk for a love that defies calculation.

S U S A N B R I A N T E is the author of *Pioneers in the Study of Motion* and *Utopia Minus*. She is an associate professor of Creative Writing at the University of Arizona.

AHSAHTA PRESS

NEW SERIES

1. Lance Phillips, *Corpus Socius*
2. Heather Sellers, *Drinking Girls and Their Dresses*
3. Lisa Fishman, *Dear, Read*
4. Peggy Hamilton, *Forbidden City*
5. Dan Beachy-Quick, *Spell*
6. Liz Waldner, *Saving the Appearances*
7. Charles O. Hartman, *Island*
8. Lance Phillips, *Cur aliquid vidi*
9. Sandra Miller, *oriflamme.*
10. Brigitte Byrd, *Fence Above the Sea*
11. Ethan Paquin, *The Violence*
12. Ed Allen, *67 Mixed Messages*
13. Brian Henry, *Quarantine*
14. Kate Greenstreet, *case sensitive*
15. Aaron McCollough, *Little Ease*
16. Susan Tichy, *Bone Pagoda*
17. Susan Briante, *Pioneers in the Study of Motion*
18. Lisa Fishman, *The Happiness Experiment*
19. Heidi Lynn Staples, *Dog Girl*
20. David Mutschlecner, *Sign*
21. Kristi Maxwell, *Realm Sixty-four*
22. G. E. Patterson, *To and From*
23. Chris Vitiello, *Irresponsibility*
24. Stephanie Strickland, *Zone : Zero*
25. Charles O. Hartman, *New and Selected Poems*
26. Kathleen Jesme, *The Plum-Stone Game*
27. Ben Doller, *FAQ:*
28. Carrie Olivia Adams, *Intervening Absence*
29. Rachel Loden, *Dick of the Dead*
30. Brigitte Byrd, *Song of a Living Room*
31. Kate Greenstreet, *The Last 4 Things*
32. Brenda Iijima, *If Not Metamorphic*
33. Sandra Doller, *Chora.*
34. Susan Tichy, *Gallowglass*
35. Lance Phillips, *These Indicium Tales*
36. Karla Kelsey, *Iteration Nets*
37. Brian Teare, *Pleasure*
38. Kirsten Kaschock, *A Beautiful Name for a Girl*
39. Susan Briante, *Utopia Minus*
40. Brian Henry, *Lessness*
41. Lisa Fishman, *FLOWER CART*
42. Aaron McCollough, *No Grave Can Hold My Body Down*
43. Kristi Maxwell, *Re-*
44. Andrew Grace, *Sancta*
45. Chris Vitiello, *Obedience*
46. Paige Ackerson-Kiely, *My Love Is a Dead Arctic Explorer*
47. David Mutschlecner, *Enigma and Light*
48. Joshua Corey and G.C. Waldrep, eds., *The Arcadia Project*
49. Dan Beachy-Quick and Matthew Goulish, *Work from Memory*
50. Elizabeth Robinson, *Counterpart*
51. Kate Greenstreet, *Young Tambling*
52. Ethan Paquin, *Cloud vs. Cloud*
53. Carrie Olivia Adams, *Forty-one Jane Does*
54. Noah Eli Gordon, *The Year of the Rooster*
55. Heidi Lynn Staples, *Noise Event*
56. Lucy Ives, *Orange Roses*
57. Peggy Hamilton, *Questions for Animals*
58. Stephanie Strickland, *Dragon Logic*
59. Rusty Morrison, *Beyond the Chainlink*
60. Tony Trigilio, ed., *Elise Cowen: Poems and Fragments*
61. Kathleen Jesme, *Albedo*
62. Emily Abendroth, *]EXCLOSURES[*
63. TC Tolbert, *Gephyromania*
64. Cody-Rose Clevidence, *Beast Feast*
65. Michelle Detorie, *After-Cave*
66. Lance Phillips, *Mimer*
67. Anne Boyer, *Garments Against Women*
68. Susan Tichy, *Trafficke*
69. Mary Hickman, *This Is the Homeland*
70. Brian Teare, *The Empty Form Goes All the Way to Heaven*
71. Gabriel Gudding, *Literature for Nonhumans*
72. Susan Briante, *The Market Wonders*

AHSAHTA PRESS

SAWTOOTH POETRY PRIZE SERIES

2002: Aaron McCollough, *Welkin* (Brenda Hillman, judge)

2003: Graham Foust, *Leave the Room to Itself* (Joe Wenderoth, judge)

2004: Noah Eli Gordon, *The Area of Sound Called the Subtone* (Claudia Rankine, judge)

2005: Karla Kelsey, *Knowledge, Forms, The Aviary* (Carolyn Forché, judge)

2006: Paige Ackerson-Kiely, *In No One's Land* (D. A. Powell, judge)

2007: Rusty Morrison, *the true keeps calm biding its story* (Peter Gizzi, judge)

2008: Barbara Maloutas, *the whole Marie* (C. D. Wright, judge)

2009: Julie Carr, *100 Notes on Violence* (Rae Armantrout, judge)

2010: James Meetze, *Dayglo* (Terrance Hayes, judge)

2011: Karen Rigby, *Chinoiserie* (Paul Hoover, judge)

2012: T. Zachary Cotler, *Sonnets to the Humans* (Heather McHugh, judge)

2013: David Bartone, *Practice on Mountains* (Dan Beachy-Quick, judge)

2014: Aaron Apps, *Dear Herculine* (Mei-mei Berssenbrugge, judge)

2015: Vincent Toro, *Stereo. Island. Mosaic.* (Ed Roberson, judge)

This book is set in Apollo MT type and Abadi MT Condensed Light
with Bauer Bodoni titles
by Ahsahta Press at Boise State University.
Cover design by Quemadura.
Book design by Janet Holmes.

AHSAHTA PRESS

2016

JANET HOLMES, DIRECTOR

ASHLEY BARR

DENISE BICKFORD

PATRICIA BOWEN, *intern*

KATIE FULLER

ZEKE HUDSON

COLIN JOHNSON

INDRANI SENGUPTA